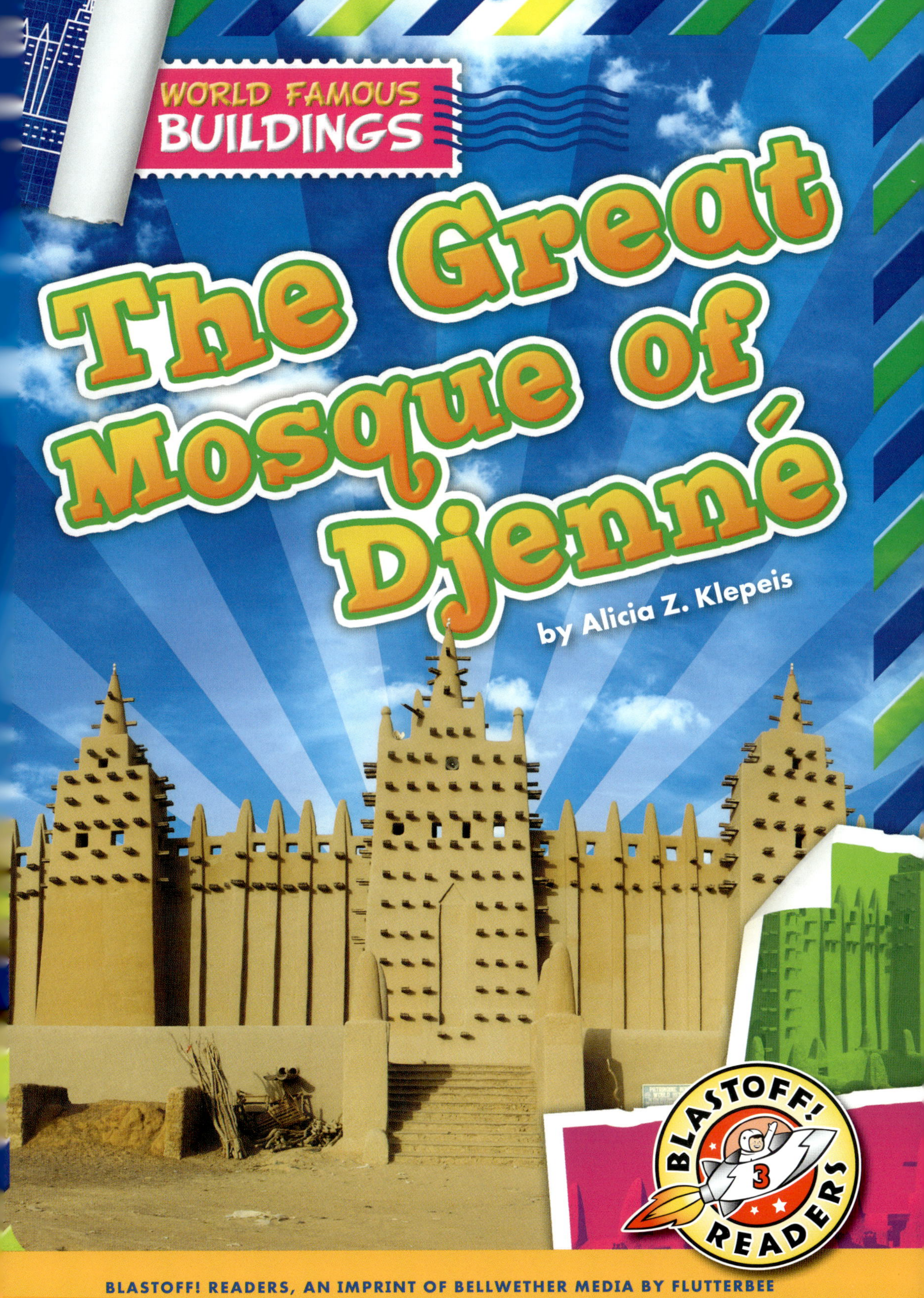

BLASTOFF! READERS, AN IMPRINT OF BELLWETHER MEDIA BY FLUTTERBEE

Blastoff! Readers are carefully developed by literacy experts to build reading stamina and move students toward fluency by combining standards-based content with developmentally appropriate text.

LEVELS

Level 1 provides the most support through repetition of high-frequency words, light text, predictable sentence patterns, and strong visual support.

Level 2 offers early readers a bit more challenge through varied sentences, increased text load, and text-supportive special features.

Level 3 advances early-fluent readers toward fluency through increased text load, less reliance on photos, advancing concepts, longer sentences, and more complex special features.

★ **Blastoff! Universe**

Reading Level

Grade K

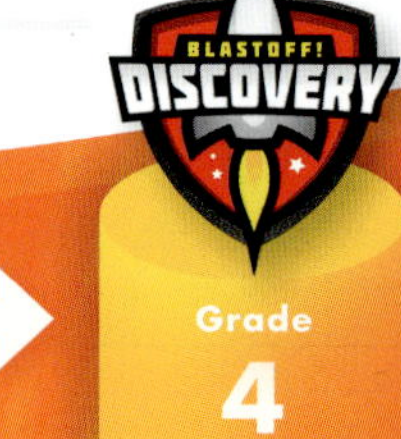

Grades 1–3

BLASTOFF! DISCOVERY

Grade 4

This edition first published in 2026 by Bellwether Media, Inc.

For information regarding permission, write to Bellwether Media, Inc., Attention: Permissions Department, 3500 American Blvd W, Suite 150, Bloomington, MN 55431.

Library of Congress Cataloging-in-Publication Data is available at www.loc.gov or upon request from the publisher.

ISBN: 9798893048070 (hardcover)
ISBN: 9798893049077 (ebook)

Editor: Betsy Rathburn Designer: Laura Sowers

Printed in the United States of America, North Mankato, MN.

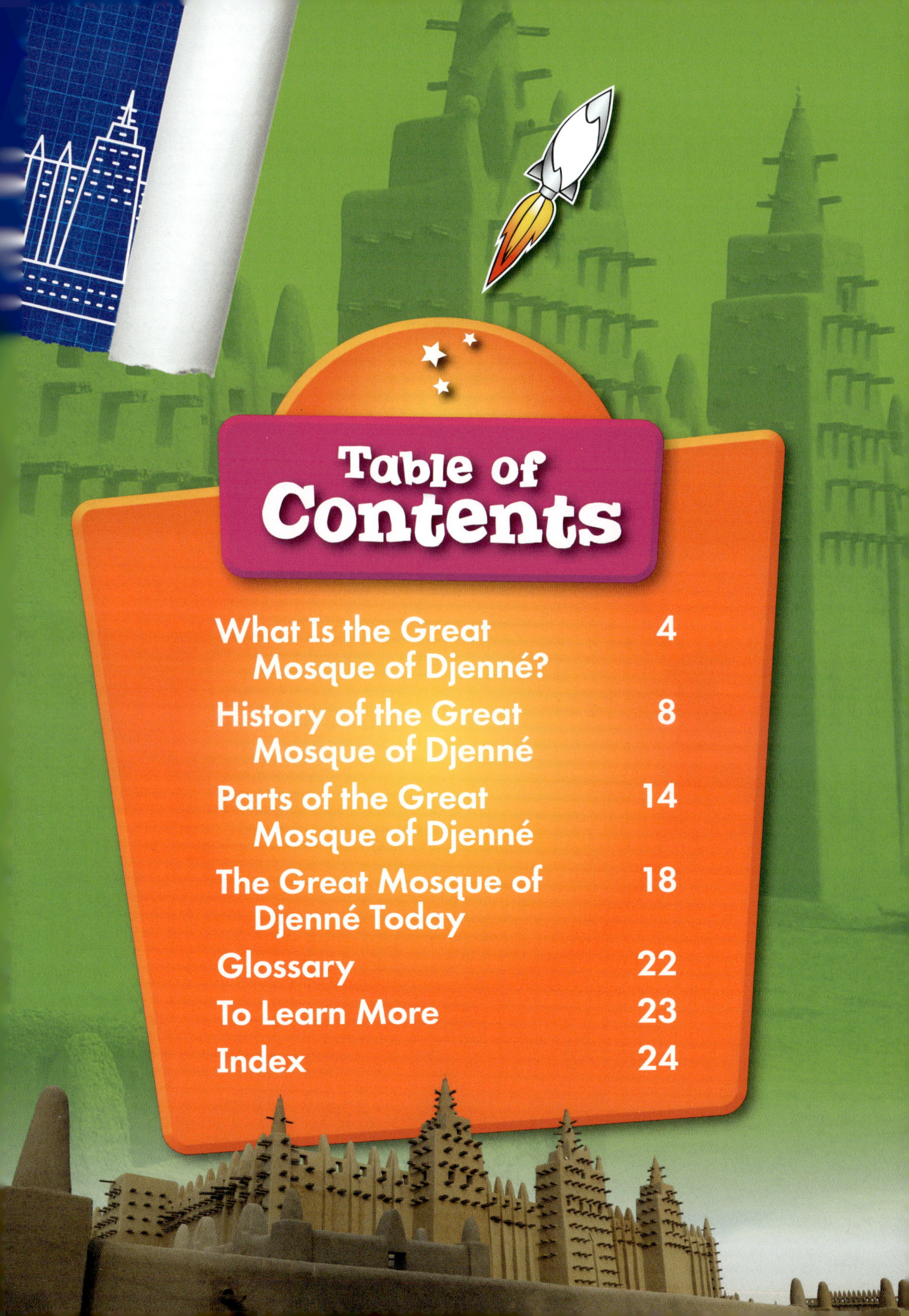

Table of Contents

What Is the Great Mosque of Djenné?

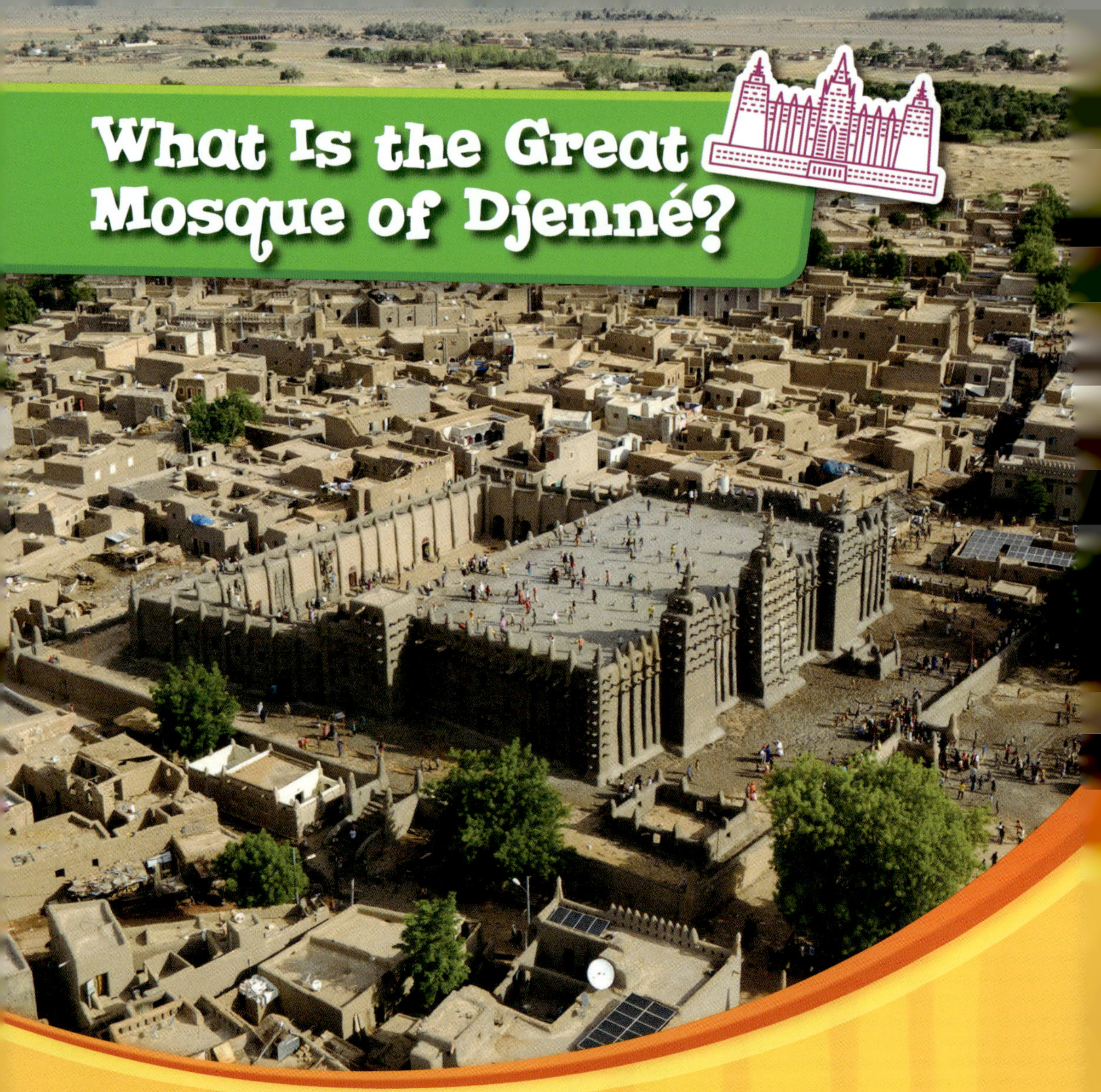

The Great **Mosque** of Djenné is a landmark in West Africa. It rises above the city of Djenné in Mali.

It is the world's biggest mud brick building.

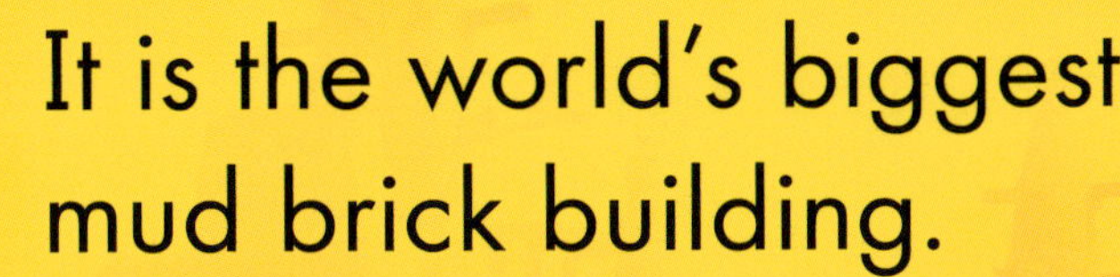

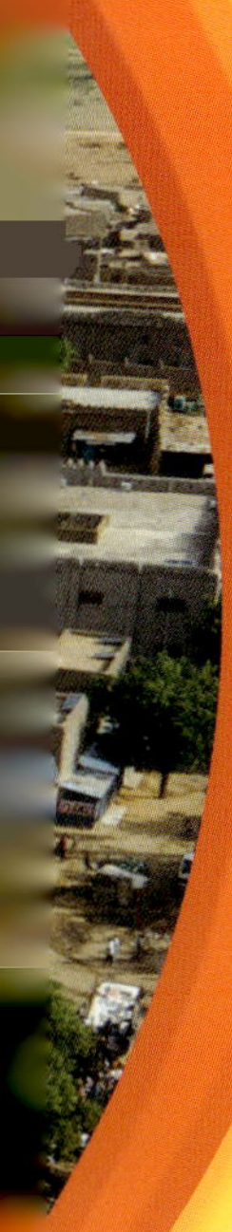

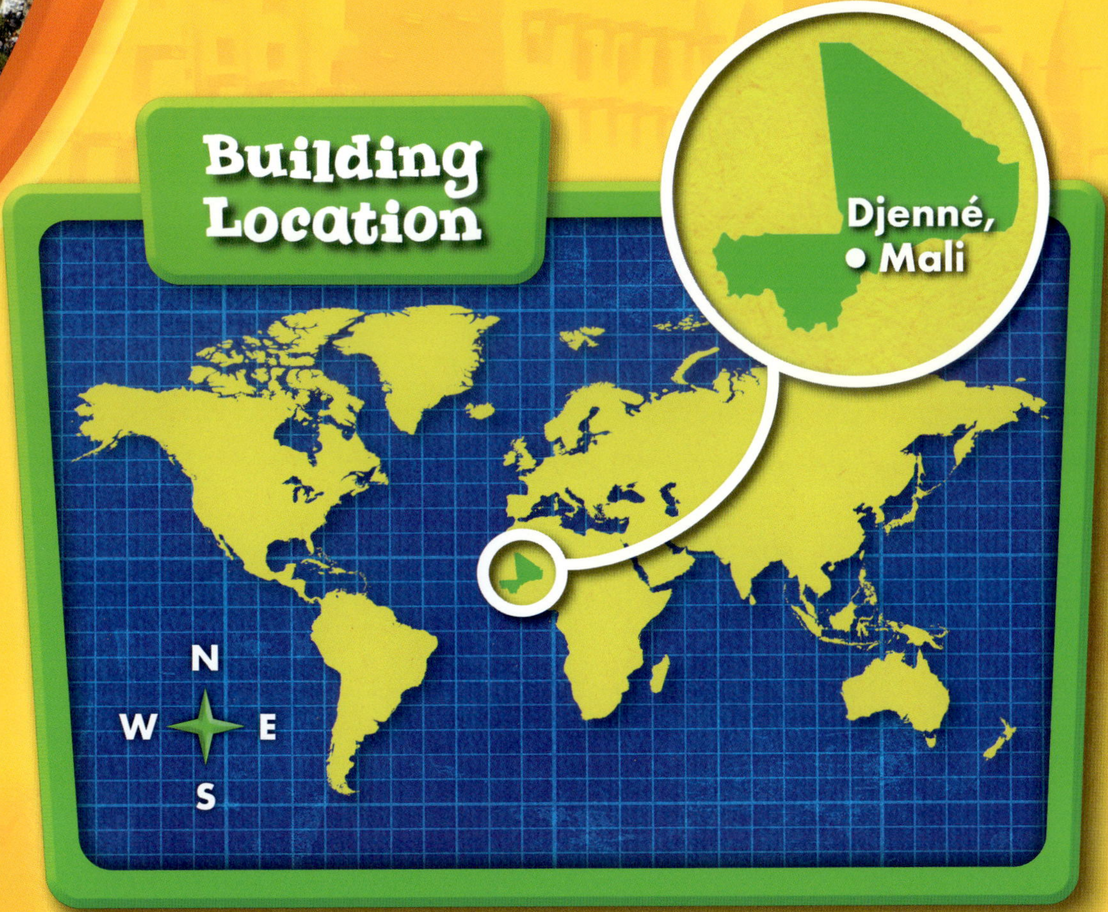
Building Location
Djenné, Mali
N
W
E
S

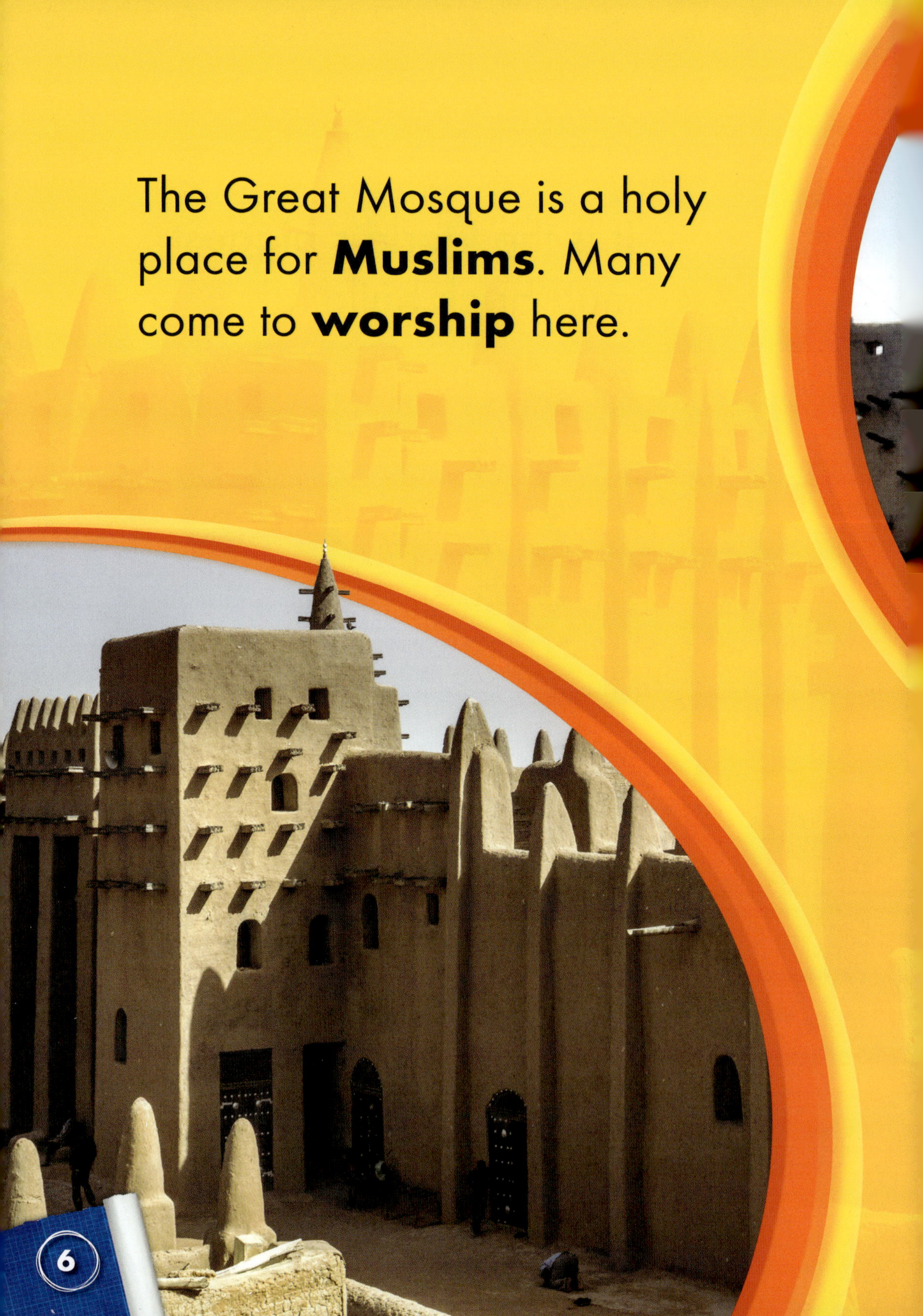

The Great Mosque is a holy place for **Muslims**. Many come to **worship** here.

Tourists also visit the site. They learn about its history and **architecture**.

History of the Great Mosque of Djenné

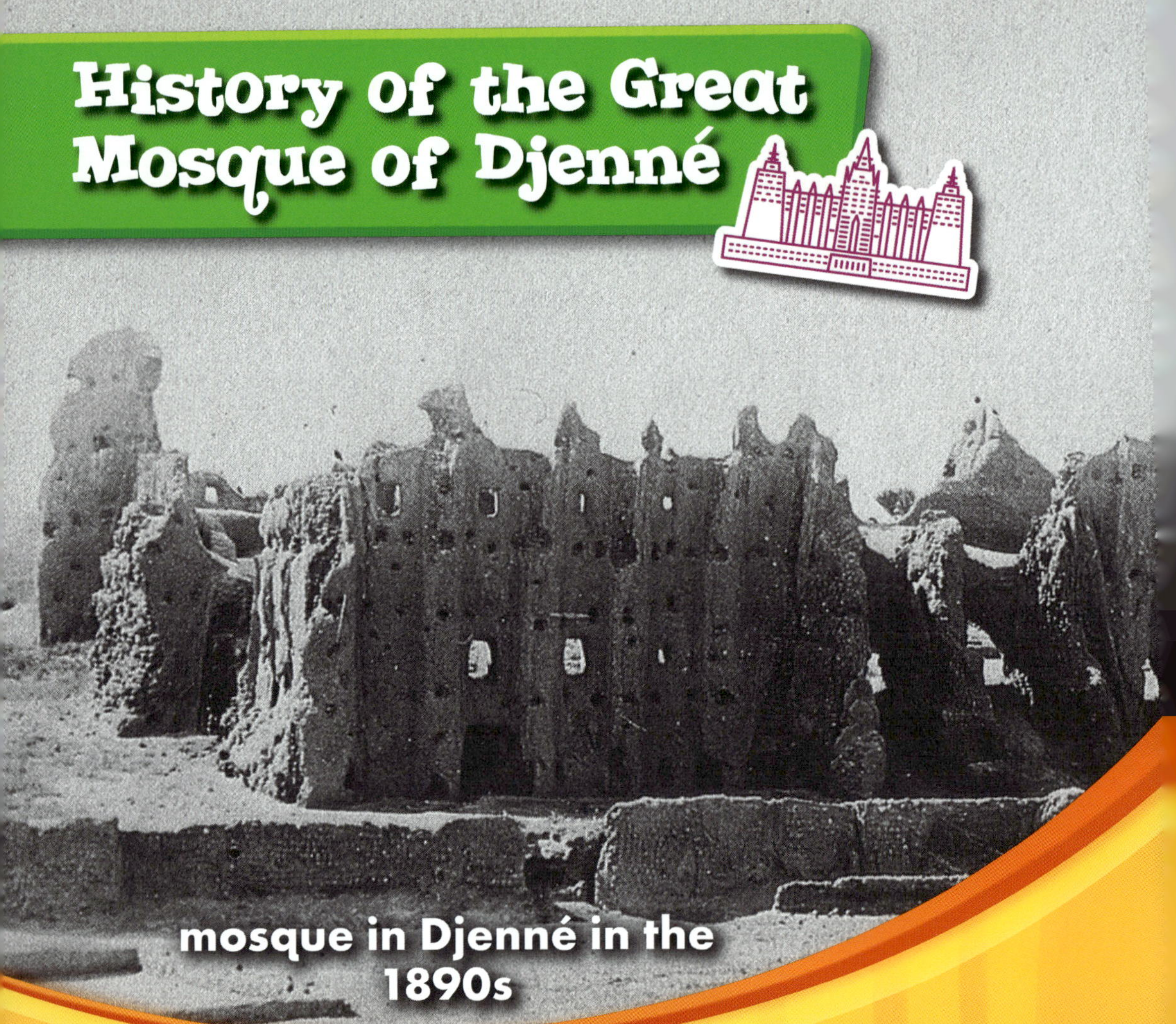

mosque in Djenné in the 1890s

Djenné was part of the **Mali Empire**. The city's first mosque was built in the 1200s. Workers replaced it with a simpler mosque in the 1830s.

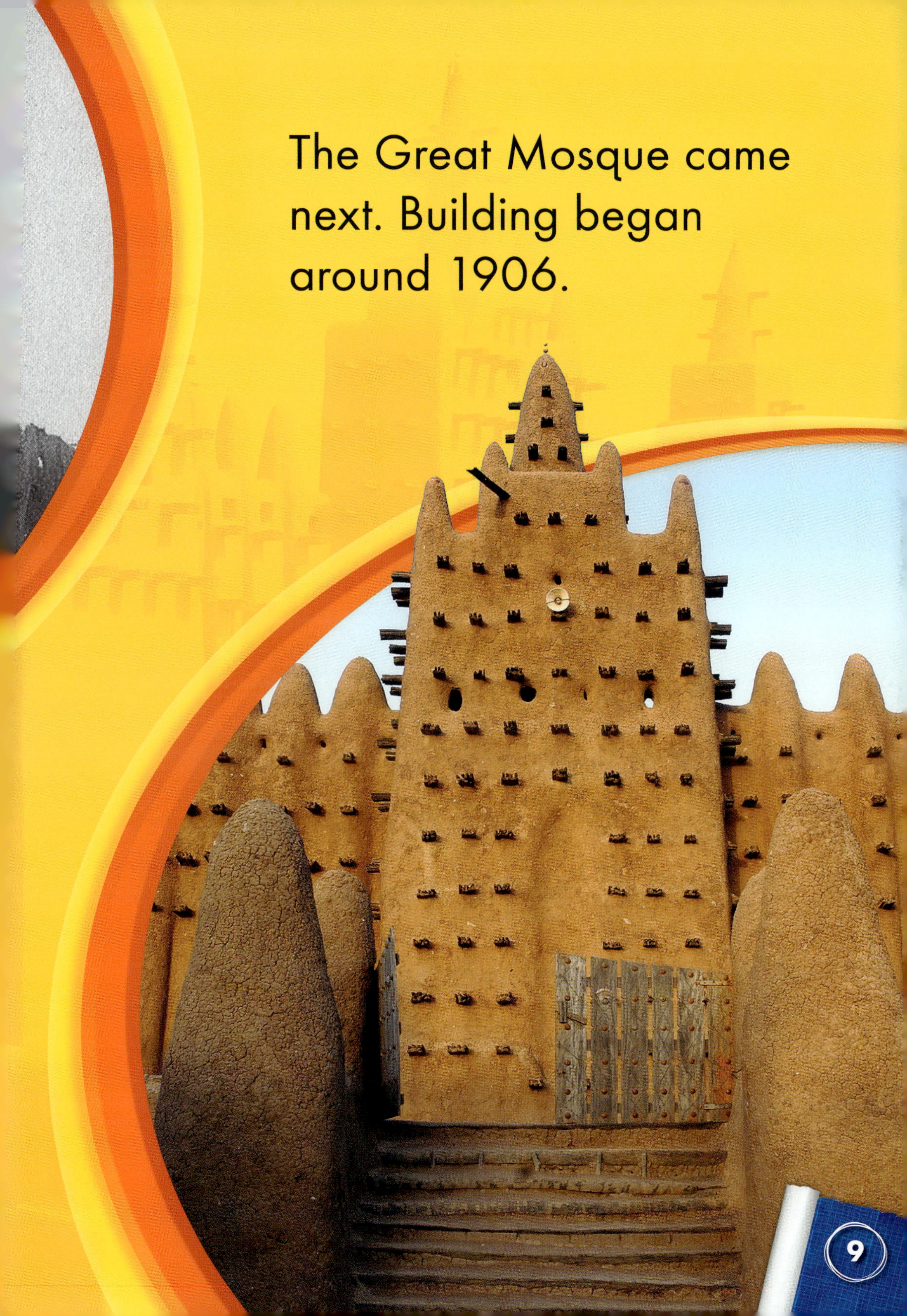

The Great Mosque came next. Building began around 1906.

Djenné stands between two rivers. This area is on a **floodplain**.

Crews built a mud brick platform under the mosque. It keeps the building safe from flooding.

The Great Mosque is mainly made of **banco**. Soil and water are mixed with other materials.

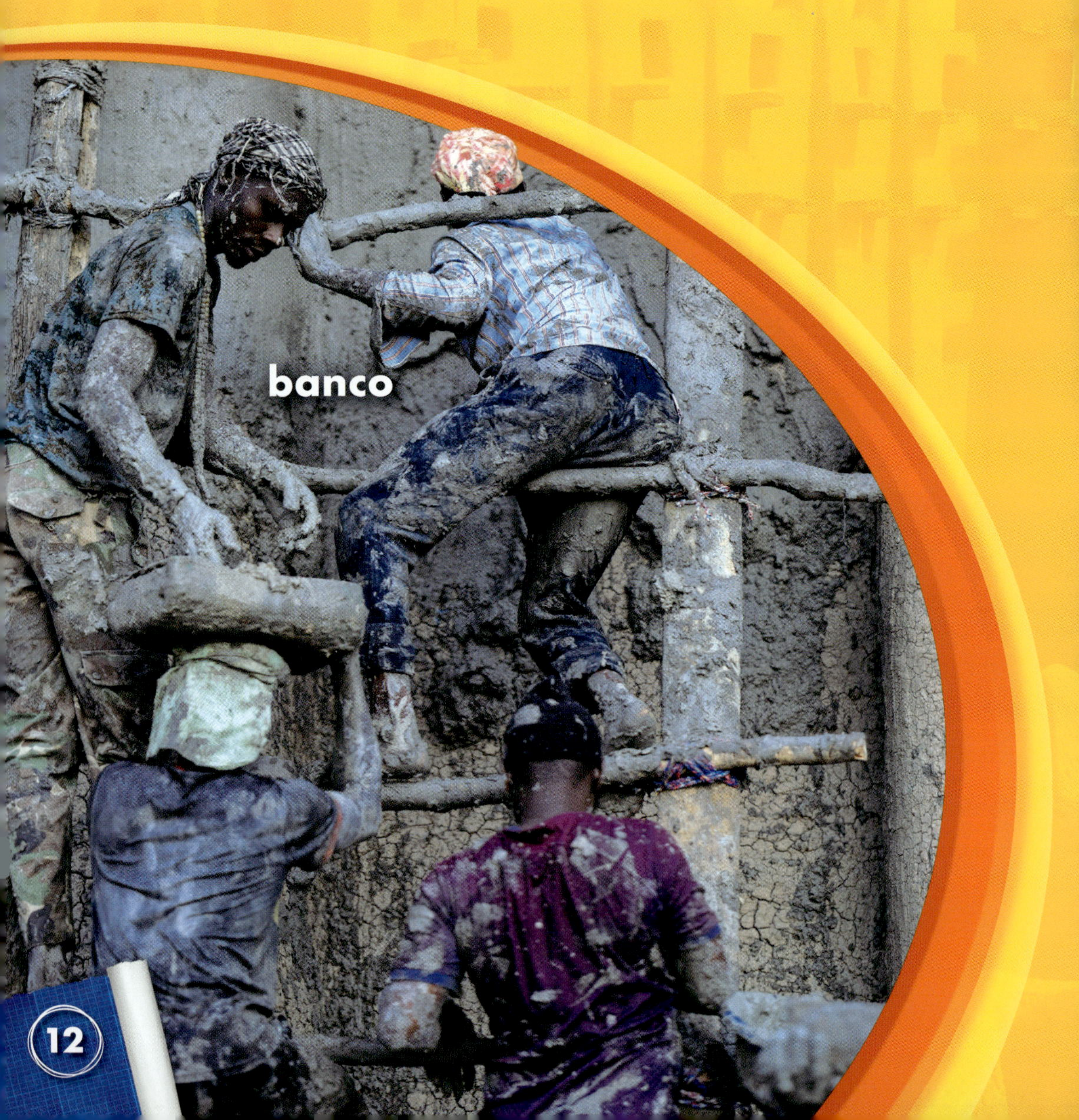

Workers formed this mixture into bricks. They also spread it like **plaster** across the building's surface.

Parts of the Great Mosque of Djenné

Thick mud walls keep the mosque cool. Palm wood stakes stick out from the walls.

Three **minarets** stick out from an outer wall. Each ends in a **spire**. Ostrich eggs top the spires!

Amazing Minarets

What They Are	tall towers with spiral staircases inside
Purpose	a religious leader climbs them to call people to prayer

The mosque has a large prayer hall. It can hold about 3,000 people!

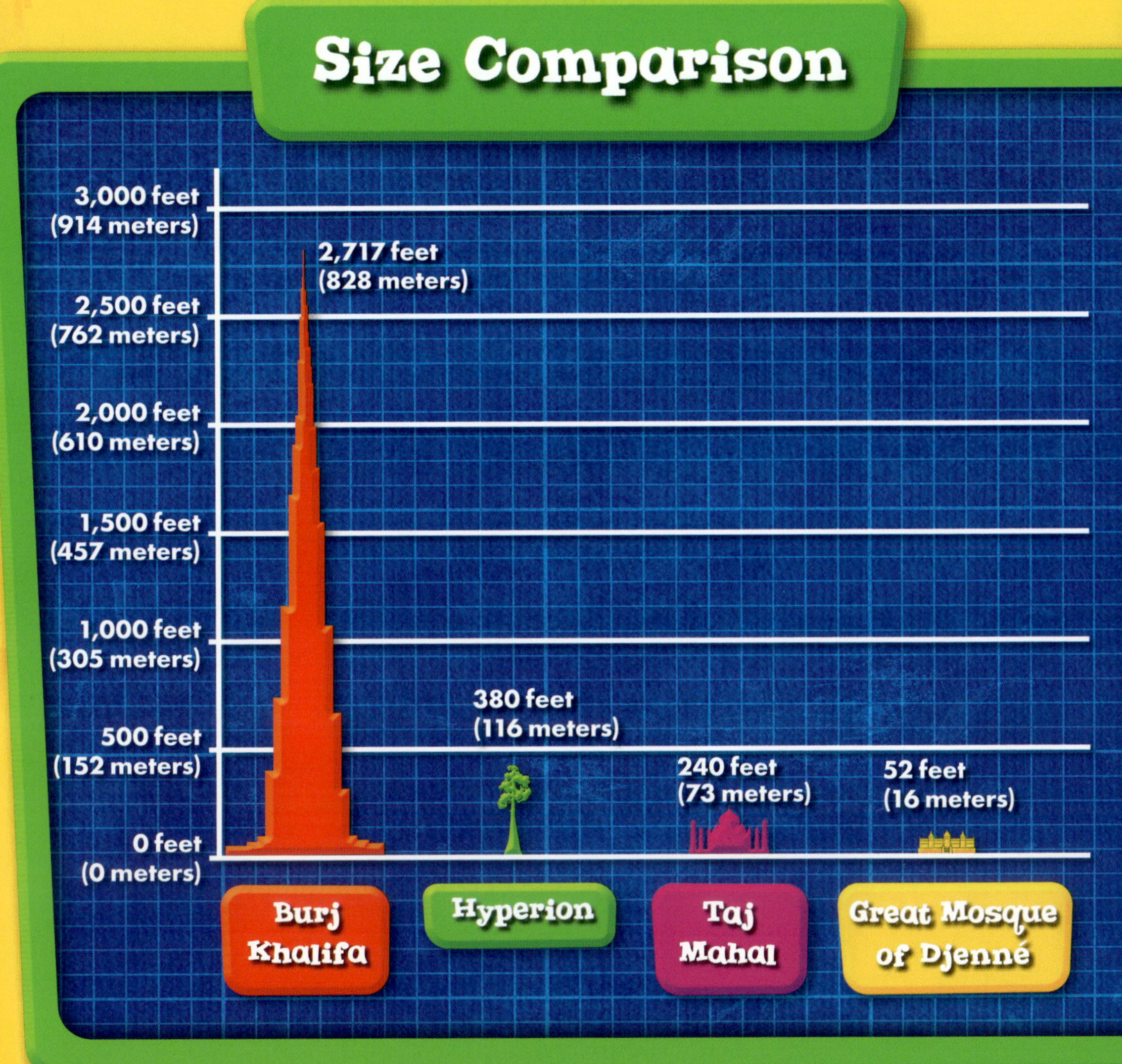

Ninety wooden pillars support the prayer hall's roof. Roof **vents** let in fresh air.

The Great Mosque of Djenné Today

The mosque's mud walls crumble and crack. The community has a festival each year. People add new banco.

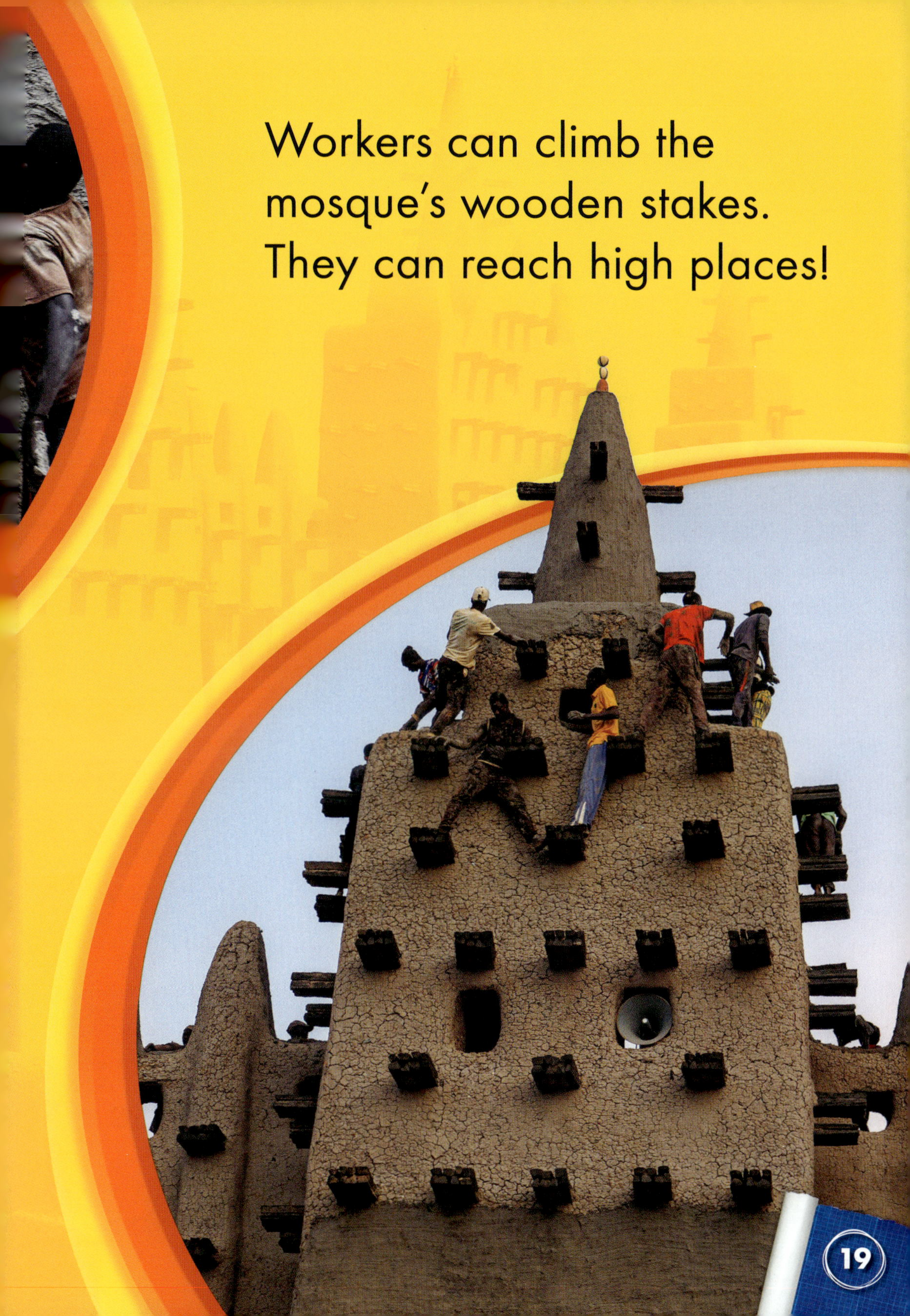

Workers can climb the mosque's wooden stakes. They can reach high places!

As many as 30,000 tourists once visited the mosque each year. But there has been fighting in the area. Fewer people visit.

This amazing building waits for tourists to return!

Glossary

architecture—the design and structure of buildings

banco—a building material made from claylike soil, water, grain husks, and other materials

floodplain—an area of low, flat land that floods when nearby rivers overflow

Mali Empire—a kingdom in West Africa that was powerful during the 13th through 17th centuries

minarets—tall, thin towers attached to a mosque; minarets have balconies used to call people to prayers.

mosque—a building that Muslims use for worship

Muslims—people of the Islamic faith; Muslims follow the teachings of the Prophet Muhammad as told to him from Allah.

plaster—a paste used to coat walls or ceilings that forms a smooth, hard surface when dry

spire—a pointed structure at the top of a building

tourists—people who travel to visit another place

vents—openings that let out air

worship—to show respect and love for a god

To Learn More

AT THE LIBRARY

Klepeis, Alicia Z. *Angkor Wat.* Minneapolis, Minn.: Bellwether Media, 2026.

Markovics, Joyce. *Ancient Architecture.* Ann Arbor, Mich.: Cherry Lake Publishing, 2023.

Walton, Kathryn. *Eid-Al-Fitr.* Buffalo, N.Y.: PowerKids Press, 2026.

ON THE WEB

FACTSURFER

Factsurfer.com gives you a safe, fun way to find more information.

1. Go to www.factsurfer.com.
2. Enter "Great Mosque of Djenne" into the search box and click 🔍.
3. Select your book cover to see a list of related content.

Index

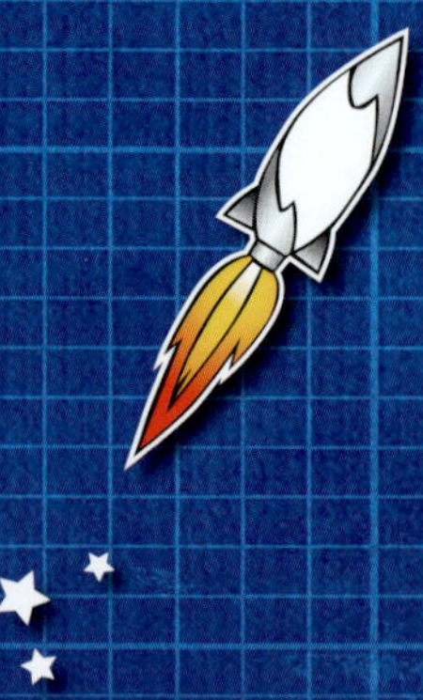

The images in this book are reproduced through the courtesy of: Watch The World, front cover; michelealfieri, front cover (inset 1); vecchiad, front cover (inset 2); piccaya, pp. 3, 23; OUSMANE MAKAVELI/ Contributor/ Getty Images, pp. 4-5, 12, 19; Torsten Pursche, p. 6; Claudiovidri, pp. 6-7; Albert Rousseau/ Wikipedia, pp. 8-9; trevkitt, p. 9; oversnap, pp. 10-11; Marco Destefanis/ Alamy Stock Photo, pp. 13 (banco), 14; sorrapongs, p. 13 (wood); pauli197, p. 13; Arterra/ Contributor/ Getty Image, pp. 14-15; Donhype, p. 15; Eye Ubiquitous/ Alamy Stock Photo, p. 16; Anadolu/ Contributor/ Getty Images, pp. 18-19; Gavin Hellier/ Alamy Stock Photo, pp. 20-21.